Praise For I NEED

MW01205535

"The journey
is one that must be taken. It is walking down the path of
life—a road already taken—with a friend who understands.
It is sharing Chocolates & Champagne in a way only those
who have walked a similar path can do—a journey…"
—Dorothy Martin-Neville, Founder & President
The Institute of Healing Arts & Sciences, LLC
Bloomfield, CT
www.instituteofhealing.com

"Absolutely fabulous! Beautifully written! Very uplifting,
inspirational book filled with laughter, tears, and just so full
of love! Bravo!"
—Valerie DeVito, Hair Stylist/Master Color Specialist

"I enjoyed this so much I read it twice!"
—Sharon Lewis, Senior Director of Member Services
YMCA, CT

"It takes talent to see the big picture, break it down, to make
an emotional experience simplistic, then spin it into a poem,
then deliver a pearl of wisdom in one verse. Loved it!"
—Katie Coleman, Mother

"I would buy it for my mother, daughter, and girlfriends!"
—Linda Pressman, Personal Trainer – Fitness Expert

Needless to say—I LOVED IT!
"You have lived a rich and full life with many more stories
and poems to come! Thank you."
—Linda Downey, Art Teacher—Norwalk, CT

2/10/07

To Carol,

Enjoy!

Kathy

I NEED A FACE-LIFT!
(Spiritually Speaking)

Thirty-One Days To Magnify Your Inner Beauty

A Step-By-Step Guide

Kathleen J. Dolan

Lulu.com

I NEED A FACE LIFT!

(Spiritually Speaking)

Kathleen J. Dolan

Copyright © 2007 by Kathleen J. Dolan
ISBN 978-1-4303-0142-4
Published by Lulu.com

Author Contact and Web Page Address:
www.kathleenjdolan.com

Cover design by Baker Graphics, Inc.
Cover photograph by Meri Wayne

If you are unable to order this book from your
local bookseller, you may order directly from
the publisher.

Manufactured in the United States of America

<u>*Dedication*</u>

To The Memory of My Mother

Eileen Mary Dolan

My Abiding Spiritual Mentor

What can we tell about mothers,
That hasn't already been told?
Volumes of books have been written,
Going back to the days of old.

This is what sets my mother apart,
From many of those preceding:
With an artist's touch, she molded my heart,
While her own—was silently bleeding.

CONTENTS

Contents

INTRODUCTION

What is the difference between a *physical* face-lift and a *spiritual* face-lift? Could it be that a *spiritual* face-lift is all you really need? What's interesting to observe is that one may directly affect the other. People may want to ask the following questions:

- What can a *spiritual* face-lift do that a *physical* one cannot?
- How can the one have an effect on the other?
- How much does it cost?
- With a *spiritual* face-lift, what are the benefits?
- Does it hurt?
- Do you need anesthesia?
- How long is the recovery time?
- Can you go to work after?
- Is it guaranteed to last?
- What kind of doctor will perform this?

The following pages will answer all of these questions—in fact, you can read this entire book in just about 45 minutes if you want to! And when you've finished, take a good look in the mirror—you've just experienced a *spiritual* face-lift!

It doesn't hurt!

BEGIN HERE:

No Anesthesia Required!

One

KATHLEEN J. DOLAN

…and I could do anything I wanted to.

ANYONE FOR CHOCOLATE?

What a momentous occasion to turn FIFTY!

THE BIG FIVE—OH!

At 9:00 a.m. I poured my first glass of champagne. Why not? It isn't every day you turn FIFTY! I gazed across the kitchen table and saw a big box of chocolates. It was the gift my sister Diane mailed me from Chicago. What could be better than to have *Champagne and Chocolates* for breakfast? With gusto, I tore off the wrapping paper and removed the cover. Oh, what heaven—all those delicious chocolates staring at me! After all, this was my special birthday and I could do anything I wanted to.

So—I ate the whole box.

Then—there was the morning after!

KATHLEEN J. DOLAN

THE MORNING AFTER

"Everything in moderation,"
That's what Mom would say.
But now that I turned FIFTY,
Things would be my way.

I saw the box of CHOCOLATES,
And boldly ate each piece.
Then landed in the doctor's office,
Begging for relief!

"Intestines blocked," said the Doc.
"Whatever did you eat?"
You see, it was my Birthday.
I merely had some SWEETS.

For three long days, I paid the price
With pain and misery.
So Mom was right, to my surprise,
She still knew more than me!

DAY 1

Listen to the wisdom of others.

Two

Who was that old looking woman?

ONE QUICK LOOK IN THE MIRROR ...

At 2:30 in the morning I woke up—couldn't sleep. My husband had gone on a golfing trip to Florida. Our big, Connecticut house was set far back off the road, and the backyard was a forest of 100-foot tall ash trees. When the wind blew, the trees swayed, the house creaked—and it sounded eerie.

So, I slowly got out of bed and moseyed into the bathroom. Innocently, I took one quick look in the mirror. Then I did a double take! Who was that old looking woman? *Oh no!* I said to myself, *I look just like my Mother!*

Granted, it was 2:30 in the morning, but I never looked this bad before. The person I saw in the mirror was seriously in need of a face-lift—and more frightening than the dark circles under my eyes, was the sullen expression on my face. That's when the mirror revealed a startling, hidden truth: It wasn't a physical face-lift I needed—it was a *spiritual* one!

I crawled back into my warm bed, puffed up the pillows, and reached for a paper and pen on the nightstand. In a groggy state, I jotted down a list of all the steps that must be taken for a face-lift. The woman that I saw in the mirror needed one for sure...

... ON THE INSIDE THAT IS!

KATHLEEN J. DOLAN

FACE-LIFT

My face needs a lift,
But not by a surgeon.
The lift that it needs
Must come through conversion!

Conversion to laughter,
Conversion to praise,
Conversion to singing,
And changing my ways!

These are the things
That are needed to place
A permanent SMILE and
LIFT to my face!

DAY 2

Decide to make a change.

Three

…we would have eaten *liver*…

MY SISTER DIANE

Diane, the one who sent me those chocolates, was two years ahead of me in school. We were very close growing up, and she would come home daily to teach me everything she learned in school that day. As a result, when I entered first grade, I knew all the readers, all the spelling tests, the entire math—everything there was. After only six weeks in first grade, they promoted me to second grade; but now my personal tutor became too busy to help me. It didn't take long to turn into a "C" student and blend in with the crowd. Isn't it interesting what little children can learn from one another?

My sister and I were inseparable, though. I can remember the time when we were about pre-school age. At breakfast, my mother would lift the two of us up and seat us side-by-side at the edge of the kitchen table—we loved having our legs and feet dangle in the air. With one big bowl of oatmeal in her left hand, and one big spoon in her right hand, my mom would feed us each a mouthful at a time—all the while telling us a *fascinating story;* this was the only way she could get us to eat the oatmeal. Coincidentally, her *fascinating story* would always end when the oatmeal was gone.

And oh—were those stories intriguing! She'd have us so captivated by them that we would have eaten *liver* just to hear what might happen next. They were full of drama, and excitement, and incredible imagination. Each morning it would be a new story. And that's how the day began: oatmeal and a story.

Diane and I still have a special relationship, and to this day, it hasn't changed. Hands down—she's still the best teacher I ever had. And what about Mom? Well—of course, she was the Mother of all Teachers—and she sure knew how to sell a bowl of hot oatmeal!

KATHLEEN J. DOLAN

BEST SISTER

Sometimes we'd play dress-up,
And then we'd play school,
And then we'd play dolls,
As we sat on a stool.

But when she played "teacher,"
I had to behave.
She told me to listen
Or I'd get a bad grade!

I obeyed everything
She taught me to do,
My very best teacher
And BEST SISTER, too!

DAY 3

*The people closest to us have lessons
to teach us. Pay attention and listen up!*

Four

…all I could do was stare at the clock…

SCHOOL DAYS – SCHOOL DAYS

The study hall was unusually quiet—so quiet that you could hear the other students breathing and the clock ticking. *What could I possibly write about?* The assignment was due in just about a half-hour.

At 16, it was my junior year of high school, and the English teacher assigned a poem to be composed by each student in class. The poems would then be submitted to the *National Anthology of High School Poetry*. From there, only a selected few would be accepted for print. I had never written a poem before—and I was panicking to come up with an idea.

Oh, how I hated deadlines; oh, how I hated doing homework! Another five minutes passed and all I could do was stare at the clock—and that blankity-blank piece of paper in front of me. Then, like lightening—in the mini-span of a second—an inspiration crashed into my head. *I got it; I got it!* I shrieked to myself. *I'll just write about what I'm thinking!*

And that's how my poem ended up in the *National Anthology of High School Poetry.*

KATHLEEN J. DOLAN

CLOCKS

Sometimes I wish there wouldn't be,
A clock that's always rushing me.
When I look upon the wall,
I often hope that it would stall!

It's rush-rush here,
And rush-rush there,
Rush-here, rush-there,
Rush-rush everywhere!

There's never time to take a breath.
The day I do will be my death.
At night I hear it tick, tick, tick.
A sound that makes me sick, sick, sick!

Some day I'll hit it with a ROCK!
And then there will be no more CLOCK!

DAY 4

Follow your inspirations.

Five

KATHLEEN J. DOLAN

...I had never seen her
before, and I never
saw her again.

AN ANGEL IN THE MIDST

Sad to say at 23, I wasn't very punctual. For the third time in a week, I had missed the last rush-hour train into downtown Chicago. Certainly, I was running out of excuses to tell my boss.

On this particular morning, as I stood on a chilly train platform in Elmhurst, Illinois, I was filled with anger at myself for missing that stupid train. Upset because of running out of the house in such a hurry—nothing I wore matched; my hair was a mess; I was hungry, and only half of my makeup was on—I felt disheveled, disorganized, and thoroughly disgusted with myself! I was so frustrated—it was all I could do to hold back tears.

As I looked toward my right, I saw a small, young woman at the edge of the platform. She caught my eye and I could see that she had Down syndrome. Slowly she walked straight up to me, smiled, and said: "You look so pretty today." Again she smiled, and quietly proceeded down the platform.

The rage inside me halted; my thoughts abruptly hushed. During the year of commuting on the train, I had never seen her before, and I never saw her again. I believe she was *an Angel in the midst.*

KATHLEEN J. DOLAN

A MISSED TRAIN

An Angel came to greet me
At the platform of the train.
Her mission was to bring me
New ways to not complain.

I heard within her voice
A gentle, kind direction.
She opened me to see things
In a clear and wide dimension.

Five words the Angel uttered,
Before she walked away.
Spoken in all honesty,
"You look so pretty today!"

DAY 5

Count your blessings.

Six

KATHLEEN J. DOLAN

From the words of a complete stranger…

A STRANGER ON THE BENCH

Trying to get all my paperwork together, I sat down on the bench outside the registrar's office of Elmhurst College. Not long after I met the *Angel* at the train, I decided to quit my job in downtown Chicago and return to college. Part of me was excited about going back to school after a three-year absence—and part of me was apprehensive. I had two more years to go.

Another student sat next to me on the bench. I could tell she was an older student, possibly going back after her children were in high school. For me, it seemed like it was taking forever to get through four years of college. Saving money was always a challenge.

Anyway, she was friendly and we started to chat as girls often do. Over the course of the conversation, I expressed my concern to her about having enough money to get through two more years. She volleyed back with strong conviction and said: "I've always believed that if a person really wants to do something—they'll find a way to do it!"

You might say that I just bumped into another *Angel;* but her statement so inspired me that I finished the next two years—in a year and a half—and with no financial burden! From the words of a complete stranger, I was empowered and encouraged.

KATHLEEN J. DOLAN

YES YOU CAN!

There's a sign on my refrigerator,
It only says three words.
They guide me on the road of life's
Intimidating curves.

These three words direct my path.
They give me hope and fuel,
To plan each day with confidence,
Equipped with every tool!

Here they are. They're yours to take.
This is what they say:
YES YOU CAN! YES YOU CAN!
YES YOU CAN! TODAY!

DAY 6

Make a positive impact today.
Give someone words of encouragement!

Seven

It was time to rebel!

DON'T LIE TO MAMA!

When I was 27, single, and living at home, I still was given a curfew of 1:00 a.m. to be home after dates. It was time to rebel!

One Saturday night, this boy named Ken and I were on a date, and I walked in the house about 5 a.m. The next morning my mother demanded to know where I was that late! So I lied and told her that we were at some bar on Rush Street in Chicago till 4:00 a.m. It was some famous bar and I can't recall the name after all these years.

Right after that, my mother turned on the TV and **all** the news broadcasts reported that this very bar had burned down to the ground at exactly 2 a.m.! I swear my mother was psychic—I could never get away with anything.

Now, what are the odds that this one time I told a lie to my mother—on this one particular night—that the bar would burn to the ground? The answer is simple. There are no odds. This was no coincidence.

DON'T LIE TO MAMA!

GOD KNOWS NO ODDS

You see, with God, there are no odds.
He's the only one in charge.
There's no way we can limit Him.
He's holding all the cards!

No way can we escape or run
From all our bad behavior.
For peace will never come to us
Until we find a savior.

You see, with God, there are no odds.
He custom-makes each case,
And tailors things by His decree
To render in His Grace.

DAY 7

That means—the odds are in your favor.
Trust in His mercy!

Eight

His name was "Ken."

TWAS THE NIGHT BEFORE EASTER

How did I meet my husband? Well...

It was the night before Easter and my girlfriend was home from college on spring break. I had already graduated in January, and was teaching on my first job in the inner city of Chicago. She was working on her Master's and didn't have a car—and couldn't stand being home with her parents!

So, she called me up and begged me to take her out for a drink. I felt rather sacrilegious going out the night before Easter but she coaxed me into it. We talked about men as we drove to this popular singles bar and I remember saying to her that I wanted to meet a guy who loved me for *who I was.*

When we got to the bar, we sat in a booth and we were just about the only people in the place. This young, blonde guy who was bartending came over to take our order. His name was "Ken." He took my order—and has been taking my orders ever since!

KATHLEEN J. DOLAN

BOY MEETS GIRL!

The name of the bar was **S. O. P.**
That stands for SOME OTHER PLACE.
The bartender there took one look at me
And said, "I like her face!"

He took my order, then pulled my hair
Just to get some attention.
I thought that was strange and laughed with my friend,
Now what could be his intention?

He continued pursuit and captured my heart;
We married shortly thereafter.
Blessed with two daughters; we've not been apart.
I'm still in love with my Captor!

DAY 8

Blessings can come in "any place."
Look for and expect one today!

Nine

Then again, have you ever gone to the zoo…

THINKING IN REVERSE

Ken and I were living the *American Dream*. First came the wedding, then the honeymoon, and then we bought our first home. But before we knew it, we were being transferred to Texas, and two beautiful daughters came along: Shannon and Tammy. It didn't take long for our little girls to pick up saying the word: "Ya'll."

One night Ken and I went out to dinner with some friends—I didn't realize that I was wearing my new black pants backwards. I thought the zipper was supposed to be worn in the front, but it was supposed to be worn in the back.

Now for some reason, this made me think of the time my mother wallpapered an entire room with the pattern upside-down! She never noticed that all the *Butterflies* in the wallpaper were flying toward the floor instead of "up." Of course, no one else in the family noticed either (this tells you something about our DNA).

It wasn't until months later when a cousin came to visit that we were enlightened to the situation. He was astute to the ways of nature, and looked at the wall in such a puzzling way. Then he gently asked why all the *Butterflies* were flying to the floor.

Maybe this type of reverse thinking is simply in our DNA. Then again, have you ever gone to the zoo and watched how monkeys do things? Could it be that we share something in common with them?

KATHLEEN J. DOLAN

MONKEYS IN THE ZOO

So my pants were on backwards,
But nobody knew.
And who really cares
Where the *Butterflies* flew!

But it makes quite a statement
To all who observe.
Mistakes can be funny
And even ABSURD!

So what can we learn
From this tale or two?
We're very much like
The—Monkeys in the Zoo!

DAY 9

Laugh! Relax!
Think like a monkey!

Ten

And what's worse, I'd be starving!

IT'S NEVER TOO LATE!

The water didn't look that cold, but when I put my toe in, it was freezing! It was my first day of *Adult Beginner Swimming Lessons* and at thirty-five years old, I thought I'd be the oldest person there. But I was pleased to find out there were others in their 50's and 60's! The swimming coach at Austin College was teaching the course and the place was Sherman, Texas.

The coach was a tall, confident man, and when he announced that you had to swim the full length of the Olympic-size pool in order to graduate from his class, I thought to myself—*This is going to take years.* It's true—I had swimming lessons as a child; I did know how to float, but the farthest I could swim to save my life was about ten feet. I didn't know how to breathe while taking strokes, and I had a genuine fear of deep water. But newly motivated, I wanted to swim as well as my five-year-old daughter, Shannon. So there I stood, with all the other non-swimmers, ready to jump in the shallow end—and did they ever keep that pool-water cold!

Weeks passed. I had no idea I was in such bad shape. Swimming takes a lot of stamina; I would get out of breath so easily and be completely exhausted by the time I got home from a lesson. And what's worse, I'd be starving! But, I was determined by the final class to pass the test and swim the length of that ice-cold pool. If it weren't for the constant encouragement of the coach, I might easily have quit.

Finally though, the last day arrived and he said, "OK Kathy! It's your turn now. Swim the full length of the pool. I'll be there to meet you!" Scared like a baby, with one foot, I gave myself a giant push off the side. Then, struggling with every stroke I took, gasping for air, I swam victoriously to the other end of the pool—and the coach was waiting to greet me! He said, "Great Kathy! Now swim back!" I said, *WHAT?* He shouted, "You heard what I said, swim back!" I answered—*I'm out of breath! I'm wiped out!* He demanded, "You can do it! SWIM BACK!"

And guess what? I DID IT! In fact, within a short time, I was swimming a quarter mile a day for exercise and relaxation.

KATHLEEN J. DOLAN

NEVER GIVE UP

They'll say it's too late.
They'll say you're too old.
They'll say you can't do it.
But go for the GOLD!

They'll say you're too slow.
They'll say you're not smart.
They'll say you can't do it.
But *hear* your own HEART!

They'll say you're all wrong.
They'll say you're a fool.
They'll say you can't do it.
But JUMP in that POOL!

DAY 10

Life is full of ice-cold pools.
Jump in!

Eleven

I went into the bathroom—looked in the mirror—and wept.

THE DAY I SAW HELL

There really aren't words that can describe this kind of a day. Maybe some people would say, "You just had to be there." But I wouldn't want even my worst enemy to have been there! It was a Monday and the very first day of First Grade for my Shannon. My Tammy was still only three years old and at home with my mother—and I was in surgery having my right breast removed!

I was young, only 36, but when they wheeled me out of the operating room, I became immediately many, many years older than a 36 year old woman. Cancer has a way of adding years, and years of wisdom to your life.

I felt like a little lamb that had been butchered! They had cut open my stomach just a few days earlier and removed my right ovary because of cysts. So, it felt like I had major incisions everywhere—and pain! In a day or two, I would be wheeled down to another room for a bone scan—to see if the cancer had spread. It was at that moment, it dawned on me my life could be very short. The sinking feeling in my stomach spoke volumes to my mind and soul. The word FEAR was no longer a word for me; it became a pervasive reality in my every-day existence. And what an *actress* I had to become to not let my family know what a hell I was experiencing. (There's no doubt that I've won the Oscar for this one!) While I was in the hospital, my husband accepted a promotion and a transfer, and in three weeks we were on a plane flying from Texas to Wisconsin to go house hunting. In less than 12 weeks, we were moving to another home in another state. I would have to find all new doctors, new friends, and keep up my great *Acting Job.*

One morning, three months later, as I drove to the grocery store, I asked myself the questions: *Did you really move? Did you really have cancer surgery? Did all this really happen?* Then I drove home to the quiet of an empty house—and for the very first time—I went into the bathroom—looked in the mirror—and wept.

44   KATHLEEN J. DOLAN

TEARS CAN HEAL

So I cried, and I cried, till I cried myself out.
Then I looked in that mirror and vowed with my mouth!

Never again would I shed one more tear!
The *sorrow* was finished! My vision was clear.

I had to keep going and look straight ahead,
And think of my husband and children instead.

It wouldn't be easy—the road would be tough.
But I knew I could do it—and be strong enough.

I'd take one big step—and then the next one, too.
I was scared and afraid—*but my life I'd pursue!*

DAY 11

Learn from your trials.
Move forward! Press on!

Twelve

There was this strong pull from within…

A JOURNEY THROUGH THE BIBLE

Everyone reacts differently to a crisis; no two people are exactly alike. After I had cancer surgery, I went on a deep, spiritual search. I felt intensely compelled to read the Bible. I was very familiar with the New Testament, but not so with the Old Testament. There was this strong pull from within that urged me to take a journey.

On the first of May, I opened up the Bible to *page one* and started reading. It was totally Greek to me—but I was determined to read it anyway until I finished. Day after day, it seemed like I would never understand what I was reading—but I kept on. Then, quietly and slowly, I started to comprehend things—and amazingly, I couldn't put the book down! On August the 31st, I closed the book. It was the same day to the year that I had the surgery, and I had completed the Old Testament. My fears about dying from cancer, which were so powerfully strong, were now gone! I came to the conclusion that there really was a *God*—that he obviously knew what He was doing—and if I were supposed to *stay alive* that would be just fine with me—and if I were supposed to *die*, then that would be OK, too—because He obviously knew what would be best for me.

I never worried about whether I was going to live or die after that. During those four months of reading the scriptures, I was astonished by the vivid and revealing dreams I had in the night. It seemed as though I was given insights and wisdom that were bestowed as a special gift for taking this incredible journey.

KATHLEEN J. DOLAN

AND THEN THERE WAS PEACE

There was worry and fear all over the place.
It lurked in my voice and showed in my face.
Then I went on a journey that took me to stay
In a place that was peaceful, yet not far away!

It was hidden inside me and there all the time.
It was buried beneath all the stress and the grime.
When I found it and saw what beauty was there,
I knew of no other place to compare!

This place was so calm, and gentle, and warm.
It kept me protected from every fierce storm.
I'm so glad I found this magical place.
The journey was worth it! It's there I found Grace!

DAY 12

Peace <u>can</u> be found.
Make it your goal!

Thirteen

"Mom, there's SHARKS in my room!"

SHARKS IN THE DARK

It was happening every night at 2:00 a.m. in the morning—our five year old, Tammy, crawled into bed with us! I would ask her what was wrong, and she said, "Mom, there's SHARKS in my room!" Then I would walk her back into her room and put on the light and show her that there were no SHARKS. With that, I tucked her in and kissed her goodnight. Five minutes later, she'd be back in our bed.

One morning a brilliant idea came to me out of the blue. That evening, when I tucked her into bed, we said our nightly prayers, and I gave her a very special *Flash Light*. I told her that SHARKS were afraid of the light, and that from now on, whenever she saw a SHARK in the dark, all she had to do was FLASH the light on him and he'd go away.

That's the last night Tammy ever came in our bedroom. Instead, at 2:00 a.m. in the morning, I'd see beams of light flashing through the hall as she zapped the SHARKS on the ceiling and walls. Then the light would stop, and she went fast asleep.

KATHLEEN J. DOLAN

LIGHT IN THE NIGHT

Wouldn't it be nice
If we could just go,
And flash a bright light
On the troubles we know?

And all of our fears,
And all of our dreads,
Would vanish away
From *inside* our heads!

This would be possible
For us to achieve,
If we would just choose
To TRUST and BELIEVE!

DAY 13

Life is a Choice.
Choose to "let go and let God!"

Fourteen

…she did the unthinkable!

SILENCE IS GOLDEN

All the mothers were standing around the ice-skating rink watching their children skate. I was one of them. My own daughters were twirling on the ice (inbetween falls). Figure Skating Class was about to begin, and all the young girls were warming up on the ice.

One particular mother made her way toward me. Her face looked familiar—she lived in the neighborhood; she had an earnest look on her face, and seemed like there was something important she wanted to tell me. That's when she did the unthinkable!

Out of nowhere, she positioned herself smack in front of me, and point-blank asked: "How old are you?" As you might imagine, I was taken quite off guard, and needless to say, shocked! With wit, I came back and said something like: *Oh, that's classified information.* But this woman was not at all phased by my reply, and audaciously persisted. Again, I laughed and joked: *Not even my husband knows!*

Now some people are incredibly nosey—and some people are remarkably stupid. In any event, if someone is ignorant enough to ask your age: DON'T TELL!

KATHLEEN J. DOLAN

DON'T TELL!

Roses are Red.
Violets are Blue.
Your age is *Your Business*.
Give no one a clue!

But if they should ask,
Or force you to tell,
Just *smile* through your teeth,
And wish them all well.

Now for those who insist,
Make one thing quite clear:
You'll give them the day; and the month;
But never the **YEAR!**

DAY 14

Render to Caesar the things that are Caesar's.
And keep your birthday to yourself!

Fifteen

KATHLEEN J. DOLAN

...she sure had us kids
fooled.

A DEFINITE CONFIRMATION

It was a fatal, massive heart attack—and it happened so fast.

After my mother died, I knew in my heart that she went straight to Heaven. Somehow, though, I wished that I could have some confirmation of it. Well, not long after her death, I had a very vivid dream in the night, where I saw a *grave*—and the *grave* was completely covered with *white lilies* planted in the shape of a large *cross.* I woke up remembering this unusual dream and wondered whose grave it was? A few nights later, around 3:00 a.m.—in the middle of the night—I was awakened by the strong smell of *lilies* in the bedroom. In fact, the scent was so powerful and penetrating that it caused me to sit up in the bed at once! It was overwhelming!

I knew then what the dream meant, and that my mother was truly at peace in Heaven. What a clear and definite sign it was. What a gift to me to know that the one person who had the deepest impact and meaning in my life—the very one who gave me life— was safe, protected, and OK.

When we remember the people we love, we often think of only the good things, the happy times, and the pleasant memories. But every saint has his or her human side, too. And although it's a given that my mother is a saint in Heaven, she also had the wildest Irish temper you'd ever want to see! Looking back, I can see she was all bark and no bite—but she sure had us kids fooled.

There is one thing that Mom did perfectly well. It went to the very core of her being. She taught me to pray and believe. Nothing, absolutely nothing, can take that gift away from me. It's the only gift that really keeps on giving.

KATHLEEN J. DOLAN

THAT REDHEADED LADY!

Oh what a temper Mom could display.
Like the fury of fire—don't get in her way!

Obey her command—you DO or you DIE.
And GOOD-LORD-FORBID if you ever ask WHY?

She scared me to death—sometimes I would shake.
I'd fear for my life—and pray for escape!

And that's why kids marry—and plan to leave home.
To get free of *Mama*—and be left alone!

But after all's said, and finally done,
I turned out just like her—you better RUN!

Even my hair came out just the same.
It's red and it's curly and looks like a flame!

But Oh! How I loved her—despite all her ways.
She's up there in Heaven—*and may God Be Praised!*

DAY 15

Discipline is the fabric of change and growth.
Develop spiritual discipline!

Sixteen

KATHLEEN J. DOLAN

After much pleading and drama…

A VALUABLE COUPON

The following Christmas, all that my girls wanted was a DOG. Living in cold Wisconsin at the time, winter was not the best season to get a puppy. And to top it off, I was vehemently against getting a pet! Unfortunately for me, I was the only one in the house that felt that way.

After much pleading and drama, I finally consented to getting a "dog," but only in the summertime when it would be easier to train the mutt (I mean "dog"). So, on Christmas morning the girls found a "Coupon" in their stockings that read:

"COUPON"
Good for One "DOG"
To be delivered June 1st.

A few months passed and now it was early May. I was becoming despondent thinking about the promise I had to fulfill! So—I decided to take a weekend trip for myself, and drive to Chicago to visit my sister. When I returned late that Sunday evening, I opened the side door to the house, walked in, and was greeted by a yapping 3-pound "Shih Tzu." While I was gone, my husband had taken the girls to a breeding farm and bought this **monster!** The "dog" looked at me, and I looked at him, and then he **"peed"** all over the carpet!

KATHLEEN J. DOLAN

MY DOG PEPPI

At first I kept him in his cage,
So not to see his face.
But a human baby's sound he made,
Crying in that place!

I felt so guilty and ashamed,
I ran to pick him up.
His eyes were filled with glassy tears,
I knew this was no mutt!

That day we both fell in love,
This tiny dog and me.
The sweetest thing that ever lived,
My precious, little Peppi.

DAY 16

Love can come through all creatures.
Let yourself be loved today!

Seventeen

KATHLEEN J. DOLAN

…but this is how family traditions get started.

IT MUST BE MONDAY

How did this happen? I just blinked and then they were both in high school.

I could remember when Shannon was a very active little girl. She loved to play with her Cabbage Patch Doll™ and always role-modeled the *teacher*. Tammy wanted to grow up and be a *tightrope walker* and play the *harp*. (Where did she come from?) And then there was the day when Shannon was four—she decided to jump off her dresser into a large playpen, and unfortunately broke her arm. Two years later, when Tammy turned four—she was roller-skating outside, and fell and broke her arm. Now this seemed very strange to me since my mother was four when she broke her arm, and I was four when I broke my arm—but this is how family traditions get started.

In our kitchen was an old, round oak table that my mother passed down to me a few years after we were married. Every Monday night, we would sit together as a family around that old, oak table and eat Spaghetti. Hail, rain, or shine—it didn't matter—that's what we had on Monday—Spaghetti! It started the week off in a very safe and predictable way. If everything else went wrong on a Monday, at least there was Spaghetti—and did it ever taste good!

Now—the girls were teenagers, and all through their high school years, they would come home so hungry from soccer practice, or tennis practice, or basketball. I'd hear the garage door open; Ken would be arriving home from work. He'd walk through the door taking off his tie—the dog would go nuts barking at everybody—and though there might be chaos everywhere—just like Old Faithful, there was *Spaghetti*. Of course, it must be Monday.

KATHLEEN J. DOLAN

TRADITION

Oh! The things you can do with a little Ragu!
Just throw in some beef, and an onion will do.
Then sauté some mushrooms to add to the sauce;
Sprinkle with seasoning and spoon with a toss.

Tell all of the family: *Dinner is Ready!*
Come in and sit down for Monday's Spaghetti!
Begin to say *Grace*, in a seated position,
Then Voila! You've started a FAMILY TRADITION.

DAY 17

Traditions are happy rituals.
Start one today!

Eighteen

I was privately praying to God...

A VERY SPECIAL BOAT!

It was 1994, one year after cancer surgery for the second time (this time it was ovarian cancer). My husband Ken and I were traveling in Kennebunkport, Maine and I was *privately praying* to God wondering if He would give me another *"Second Chance"* at life. Suddenly Ken saw this tourist boat and said, "Hey Kathy, let's go for a boat ride!" It was a beautiful, hot and sunny, summer day—and as we approached the boat to get on board, I realized that God had heard and answered my *private prayer*.

On the side of the boat, written in big letters, was its name…

"SECOND CHANCE"

KATHLEEN J. DOLAN

SECOND CHANCE

How clever of God
In using a boat
To deliver a message
Of *Mercy* and *Hope!*

I yearned for more time
To spend on this earth.
Then He granted it freely
With a brand-new rebirth!

God wanted most dearly
My life to enhance,
When He reached down and gave me
One more **"*Second Chance!*"**

DAY 18

Ask and you shall receive.

Nineteen

…this was a
CALL BACK!

FIFTEEN MINUTES OF FAME!

SHOW BIZ here I come! Ken's work transferred us to the East Coast and now we were living in Connecticut—just a one-hour commute from Manhattan. The girls were both off to college, and I was off to my first love—ACTING. I found myself an agent in New York, updated my Equity, SAG, and AFTRA cards, and was back in Show Business!

It's every good actor's dream to perform on Broadway. So, there I was, waiting to walk into a Call Back Audition for a big, Broadway musical! Mind you—this was a CALL BACK! Being in perfect voice, I was completely prepared and ready to go for it. I took three deep breaths and confidently waltzed into that audition-room to give "the best audition of my life!" YES! I knew I nailed it!

When the audition was over, I exited the building in an absolute daze. As if floating on three clouds—I proceeded to walk down the streets of New York. Then, while basking in this trance-like state, I wandered into a McDonald's and ordered a hot cup of tea "to go." I paid for the tea and left (like a zombie) as I continued walking for three more blocks. That's when it hit me! I paid for the "tea"—and left it on the counter!

A wife, a mother, an actress—life was good. Anyhow, so goes the tale of my illustrious *Fifteen Minutes of Fame.* I never got the job! *But OH! What glory I had for fifteen minutes!*

KATHLEEN J. DOLAN

APPLAUSE – APPLAUSE

The music played,
And the people stayed
To watch me take a bow.

The crowd kept cheering,
As I kept hearing,
You're Great! You're Good! You're WOW!

I beamed with glee!
It was clear to see,
They REALLY, REALLY, LIKED ME!

Then a **VOICE** said, *Gee!*
You forgot your "tea!"
And I laughed at myself politely.

DAY 19

Genuine applause begins from within.
Pat yourself on the back today!

Twenty

KATHLEEN J. DOLAN

I really want to be alone!

TO THE LIBRARY WE SHALL GO

It was a **VERY BAD DAY.** I decided to go to the library with a large pad of paper to *vent.* That's right—I was going to write down everything that bothered me, angered me, or whatever else was going wrong! When I entered the library, I chose the Reading Room to go into because nobody was there. There were magazines and newspapers on the shelves—and I wanted to be absolutely alone. Then I noticed this old woman in the corner, perhaps in her early nineties, very bent over with a cane. She appeared to be quite peaceful and tranquil—not at all like the inner turmoil that was going on inside me. *Darn it!* I thought to myself. *I really want to be alone! But then this is a public place and I don't own the library.*

I found myself a seat at the other end of the room with the magazines behind me, and began to write about every complaint that I could think of. In fact, I couldn't write fast enough; my pen was moving faster than a speeding bullet. Then this little old lady started walking in my direction. Her movements were very slow and deliberate. I perceived it wasn't easy for her to walk, but she had a pleasant look on her face. She was eyeing the magazines and probably wanted to get one. Of course, I didn't really want to pay any attention to her—I wanted to marinate in my miseries and just keep writing.

Soon I observed that she was standing directly behind me and was bending over to get a magazine—that's when she let out the LOUDEST FART I've ever heard! It took all the restraint that anyone could muster to keep from falling off the chair and doubling over with laughter! Then she smiled, and slowly shuffled across the room to where she came from.

KATHLEEN J. DOLAN

REACTION TO GAS

No, I wasn't repelled
By the gas that she passed.
How could I have been?
It was such a good laugh!

That little old lady
Could not even *hear*
The super-charged sound
That came from her rear!

When God needs to teach us
To lighten our mood,
It's HUMOR He uses
For a bad ATTITUDE.

DAY 20

Practice an "attitude of gratitude."

Twenty-One

Who are you striving to become?

I AM AWESOMELY PUNCTUAL!

On an August afternoon, I was sitting in a coffee shop in Westport, Connecticut. Someone had left a copy of the New York Post on the table, so I started to thumb through it.

An article caught my eye, and I began reading it. It was titled, "Affirmation Nation," written by Farrah Weinstein, and the article talked about how people today are writing daily affirmations to make positive changes in their lives—and highlighted some celebrities. The article instructed that anyone could design their own personal affirmations by writing them in the present or past tense, keeping them positive, and then writing them out ten times each morning and ten times each night. I was so impressed by this article, that I went home and wrote my first positive affirmation.

Notoriously late for every occasion, I decided that the one dramatic change I desired was to be on time. So I found a tablet of paper near the kitchen phone and wrote this statement: *I am awesomely Punctual!* Figuring my case was such an extreme one— I began writing this affirmation twenty times each morning, and twenty times each night.

WHAT a dramatic change almost instantly! I continued to write my affirmation, as the article suggested, for many weeks to follow. Since then, four years have passed and I've not been late for one thing! For me, this was a miracle. So I thought to myself: *I'd bet I could re-invent my whole person. I'd bet I could change anything I wanted to—simply by writing affirmations!*

Introspectively, I began to think about the person I wanted to become. I know that it doesn't matter what work we do—or how much money and possessions we accumulate—but only who we become as a person that matters. So, I asked myself: *Who are you striving to become?* From that one question, came forth a litany of affirmations to live by; each one designed to combat my own personal character defects. This is a life-long project. But what a pay-off: *I am awesomely punctual!*

KATHLEEN J. DOLAN

BEGIN TO AFFIRM

Decide what you want,
Then write it all down.
Declare it out loud,
In a strong, steady sound!

Affirm yourself daily!
Be constant and clear.
You'll conquer your demons,
And master your fear.

See yourself *dancing*
As life picks up steam.
And all that it takes
Is to **write down your Dream!**

DAY 21

Choose one thing you want to change or create.
Write your first "positive affirmation"—NOW!

Twenty-Two

I mean, "Who knew?"

THE COUNTRY FAIR

My friend called me up and wanted me to go with her to a Country Fair in Guilford, Connecticut. It was a gorgeous day, the sun was shinning, and I said, "OK." Honestly, it's not something that I had any interest in or would have decided to do on my own, but this is the reward you get from having many friends with varied interests; they force you to try things you've never done before.

When we arrived at the Country Fair, I was astonished to see so many different kinds of bunnies. There were white ones, and black ones, and camel-colored ones, and grey ones, and spotted ones—big ones and little ones! Then I saw cows, and goats, and sheep—and the *Flying Wallenda Family* was performing their famous tightrope act. But I still can't get over the outstanding variety of bunnies I saw that day! After all, I'm just a city-girl, so "Who knew?"

Sometimes it's good to do things totally foreign to our normal, routine stuff. How was I to know that bunnies came in different colors? I thought they were all supposed to be PINK. I mean, "Who knew?"

KATHLEEN J. DOLAN

WHAT THE BUNNIES TAUGHT ME

Variety is the spice of life
That keeps us entertained.
It nourishes the very soul,
And activates the brain.

Without it we would surely die,
Our nature longs for change.
If "boredom" is the problem,
Then who will take the blame?

It's up to us to seek and find
The beauty in creation,
Where unmatched splendor vibrates
In its awesome fascination!

DAY 22

Observe and appreciate the beauty in creation!
"You" are a part of it!

Twenty-Three

KATHLEEN J. DOLAN

…it felt so good to love them!

THEY JUST GREW UP!

That's right—they just grew up! My kids just grew up! I woke up one morning and they were gone; the house was empty. They had graduated from college—both had jobs, apartments, friends, and paychecks—and there I was!

One night in July, in the middle of the night, I started thinking about them. Call it grief; call it remorse; call it empty-nest syndrome—call it whatever you want to—anyway that night I wished that I could hold them in my arms, and squeeze them, and tell them how much I loved them. I remembered when they were little and I would wrap them in a warm blanket, tenderly caressing and kissing them. But now they were young adults; Tammy was living and working in Florida, and Shannon's wedding was four months away! *But then*, I thought to myself, *even though they're grown, I could still hold them after all. I could just use 'visual imagery' and imagine that I'm right there with them right now!*

And that's exactly what I did. I imagined that I was sitting on our couch in Connecticut and Shannon and Tammy were next to me—and I visualized that their heads were on my lap and they were wrapped in a big blanket and I hugged them tight and told them how much I loved them. And, it felt so moving and comforting to me—my eyes were watering—it felt so good to love them!

Life comes to us in a package. Inside that package lies the full gamut of every human emotion—happy, sad, glad, mad—we have good times and bad times. Sometimes life can be gentle, and sometimes it just hurts so much. It's like the beautiful rose that also has a thorn. And despite the pain, and the rain, I wouldn't miss it for anything! If life could be put into one big POT, what else do you think we would find in there?

KATHLEEN J. DOLAN

WHAT'S IN THE POT?

Is it Gold? Is it Silver?
Is it Fortune or Fame?
If life is a POT,
Is it filled with some pain?

Oh Yes, my dear friend.
That's in there, too.
The POT is a mixture
Like any good stew!

It would be too bland
If it had not a spice.
So the CHEF that prepared it
Threw in some *Dice!*

DAY 23

Roll with the punches!
Roll with the dice!

Twenty-Four

...offering a $1000 reward...

SOMEWHERE OVER THE RAINBOW

It was just a few short months before my daughter Shannon's wedding, and there were posters hanging all over our neighborhood offering a $1000 reward for a missing cat; there are a lot of wealthy people in Fairfield County, Connecticut. The cat was described as "black" with white markings.

Well, sure enough, Shannon and I saw a black & white cat lying on our front lawn. So, Shannon called the number printed on the poster, spoke to a woman who told her to give the cat some tuna fish—and she would come over immediately in her car! We hastily gave the cat some tuna fish, and Shannon started counting the $$$$$ in her head because she was absolutely certain this was *the cat!* Neither of us had ever seen this cat before in the neighborhood, and Shannon was thrilled to think that Lady Luck was shining on her. As soon-to-be Newlyweds, One-Thousand-Dollars Cash would sure come in handy!

Well… it wasn't the cat! And so we were out a can of Tuna Fish! NOW here's the point. Everyone is looking for the Pot of Gold at the end of some rainbow. Isn't that why we had the California Gold Rush? And isn't that why people keep coming back to the casinos? The Pot of Gold isn't the real prize, though. It's just an illusion! The real prize is in the journey—the journey full of hope, full of expectation, full of wonder, full of anticipation, and full of dreams!

After the whole incident was over, Shannon and I giggled with laughter. Life played a funny joke on us. Who would be next to be fooled by that CAT? No, we didn't get the Pot at the end of the Rainbow; instead we had an extra scoop of excitement added to our day.

KATHLEEN J. DOLAN

"THE SLOTS"

I wanted to "Win,"
So I put in a quarter.
A slow start for sure,
As I sipped on some water.

The casino was packed.
The machines were all ringing.
I hoped for a Jackpot,
By the end of the evening!

Four Aces came up
On my nickel machine,
And 800 coins came
Tumbling toward me!

I cashed in my POT
To see what it earned me.
But found that the FUN
Was all in the JOURNEY!

DAY 24

Live in the "present moment."
Enjoy the journey!

Twenty-Five

KATHLEEN J. DOLAN

…and *nobody* predicted it.

CAUGHT IN THE DARK

It was mid-August, 2003, and my future son-in-law found himself in the middle of New York's "Black-Out." The power had gone out the day before, and he was stuck in the city with only two dollars in his wallet (all the ATM's weren't working of course), and it was extremely hot in his New York apartment. Like hundreds of others, he was trying to catch a train out to Connecticut. Eventually, he managed to finally get a train around 1:00 p.m. that took him to a location 25 miles from our house. We drove there and picked him up for the weekend; being stranded in the hot city with no electricity, no air-conditioning, and limited train service, was no picnic!

This incident got me to thinking: *Where are all the Psychics when you need them?* If he could have been warned that this "Black-Out" was coming, he would have had cash in his pocket, and a couple of flashlights. There's truth in the old saying: *Forewarned is Forearmed; but* there was no warning and people just had to adapt. Some folks had Blackout Dinner Parties and some people were stuck in elevators! Some people panicked, while others laughed the night away at a nearby bar—in candlelight! In any event, it wasn't your ordinary weekend—and *nobody* predicted it.

KATHLEEN J. DOLAN

CRYSTAL BALL

If we could see the future,
And know what to expect,
Would life be as exciting?
Or have the same effect?

There's a reason we don't know
The things that are to come.
It adds suspense and interest
To what might be *Ho-Hum!*

So mount your horse and grab the reigns.
Sit high upon the saddle.
Prepare for bumps; prepare for rain.
We're soldiers in the BATTLE!

DAY 25

"Change" is a constant.
Prepare for it through "acceptance."

Twenty-Six

Apprehensively, I opened the lid.

DIAMONDS ARE FOREVER

The "Wedding Day" was almost two months away and things were going along very smoothly. Shannon, the Bride-to-Be, was now focusing on finding the perfect veil. Reminiscing, I could remember the beautiful long, cathedral veil my Aunt Cass made for my wedding. It was in a box somewhere in the basement along with my wedding dress. We had packed that box with us everywhere we moved—from Illinois, to Texas, to Wisconsin, and now here in Connecticut! After 30 years of marriage, I wondered what it looked like (don't think I even peeked at it in all that time).

Curious, I walked down the steps of the basement searching for the tattered box. Since it was never professionally wrapped, I wondered if there'd be a dead mouse in the box and some spiders—*thirty years* is a long time! Then I spotted the box stored under the basement steps with piles of other boxes; it was covered in dust and dirt. Apprehensively, I opened the lid. There it was—my beautiful white dress—turned solidly *Yellow*! It looked like something from the 1800's; it was so deteriorated! Then I reached to pick up the veil and to my shock, it was thoroughly disintegrated. The veil had turned to powder! At that same moment, I glanced at the sparkling diamond on my left ring finger. *Look!* I said to myself. *It's as beautiful as the day Ken placed it there!* And I'm sure it's quadrupled in price.

Some things do stand the test of time, and so did our marriage. We weathered many storms together and the marriage-knot was still holding. In the deepest crevices of my heart, I wished the same for Shannon. It was my prayer that her marriage would be rock-solid; excellent cut; and shine with the brilliance of a *"Diamond."*

KATHLEEN J. DOLAN

FLOWERS, CHOCOLATES, & DIAMONDS

What makes for a good marriage?
Do you really want to know?
Three things are all it takes,
For it to stay "aglow."

Just like a clock needs winding,
To keep it always chiming,
A marriage needs attention,
To save it from contention.

FLOWERS light the face with JOY.
CHOCOLATE is the tummy's TOY.
But here's the clue that's even better.
DIAMONDS, dear friend, are FOREVER!

DAY 26

The most precious "Diamond" is your SMILE!
Give it away! Let it sparkle!

Twenty-Seven

…who's teaching whom?

NO SURPRISE

It was no surprise when the beautiful maid-of-honor, Tammy, caught the bouquet. My little girl who wanted to grow up and become a tightrope walker and play the harp—who saw sharks in her bedroom at night—was now the same adventurous personality she always was. It was also amazing that she arranged to have her own personal harp-instructor (the lead harpist for the Naples Philharmonic Orchestra) play at her sister's wedding. Gratefully speaking though, I'm glad Tammy decided not to become a tightrope walker.

So, it seemed quite in keeping with her nature when Tammy told me she wanted to move out west to San Diego and sample life near the Pacific. Soon after she arrived, I was excited to hear about her adventures surfing in the ocean; becoming a vegan and eating raw food; and discovering the beautiful landscapes of southern California. How delighted I was deep down inside, to know that she was a natural risk-taker, grabbing life by the horns and living it! For sure, how could I expect that my free-spirited daughter would ever want to do something ordinary? So, once again, I was not surprised when she phoned and said she would soon pass her exam to become a certified, medical "Hypnotist!" And after she flew home and individually hypnotized each member of the family, I realized what a genuine gift she had—an insatiable desire to learn and explore!

After all, wasn't I the one who always told my girls to follow their dream, listen to their heart, and become whatever they wanted to? Didn't I always encourage them on? And didn't this all come back to haunt me when Tammy insisted that I follow through and write this book? "You're good, Mom. Just keep writing!"

Wait a minute! Who's teaching who? Or should I say, who's teaching whom?

BOOMERANG

I wonder if Abe Lincoln's mom,
Ever guessed what he would be?
Or the mom of Chris Columbus,
As he sailed out to sea?

It's scary when you start to think
The strength our actions have,
On the children we bring into life
As a rookie Mom and Dad.

I never knew a word or two
Could carry so much weight.
Until those words came back to me
In Tammy's grown-up face!

DAY 27

Things have a way of coming back to us.
Send out only the best!

Twenty-Eight

…a Baby Human Being!

BABY JAKE ARRIVES!

His hands were so small and delicate—his tiny long fingers opened slowly with quiet grace. It had been twenty-eight years since I held a newborn. When he was in my arms for the first time, my body was stiff and rigid, afraid that I might break him, but after two full days, the little guy was not so intimidating. As a *Grandmother* for the first time, I could only marvel at the variety of facial expressions he created, and the gentle way his little red lips would form the perfect shape of the letter "O."

He was thirteen days old when I first saw "Baby Jake" and my daughter was recovering well from her C-section. With great anticipation, my husband and I had arrived to help out and enjoy this wonderful occasion! Deep down inside me, I pondered if I could remember anything about having a baby! It all seemed so long ago and far away. Soon I realized that I had forgotten how often a baby needs to be fed, and all the sleep-deprivation that a new mother has to go through. It didn't take long to realize why motherhood is intended for the young and not the old. The physical endurance needed to operate on small amounts of sleep wipes out even the young. Feeding an infant every three hours round-the-clock gives a genuine appreciation for the word "fatigue!"

Despite all the time and effort involved, I couldn't help being overcome with the illuminating presence of such a miraculous work of art—a Baby Human Being! In my eyes, all I could see was the perfection and beauty of this glorious creature—and I helplessly fell in love with "Baby Jake." Again, I was re-affirmed of the majesty and awesomeness of God.

In one split moment, I looked into Jake's deep blue eyes and he looked into mine, and I knew what he would say if he could speak.

He would say: "I like this person—she seems nice! I think she loves me!"

KATHLEEN J. DOLAN

BABY JAKE!

How precious is my Baby Jake!
He's really mine you know.
His parents think they brought him here,
But it's prayer that made it so!

Call me any name you want:
Grandma, Gram, or Granny.
But I'm the one, who prayed him here,
So call me his "Prayer-Nanny!"

I went to Mass most every day
To pray his safe arrival.
And now he's here to bring us all
His sweet and gentle *SMILE!*

DAY 28

Prayer brings life and healing.
Become a "Prayer-Nanny!"

Twenty-Nine

What *legacy* do I pass on to him?

WHAT REALLY MATTERS?

What do I tell my new grandson, Baby Jake? What *legacy* do I pass on to him? Do I tell him about all the things I've done? Do I tell him that I've worked in a bakery, a cleaners, a grocery store, a bridal shop, and a car rental agency; that I've sold lamps at Marshall Fields, furniture at Montgomery Wards, and costume jewelry at J C Penney's? And do I tell him that I've done temp-work, modeling, acting in regional theatre, taught school in the inner city, did substitute teaching in the "burbs," worked as an Advertising Rep for the Chicago Tribune, managed an Employment Agency, conducted motivational training, and then went back to my first love of acting—did some commercials, a few Off-Broadway readings, some TV movies, and a couple of Saturday Night Lives? (I know I'm missing a few jobs along the way!) Is that what I tell Baby Jake?

But does all this really matter? Will it make any difference whatsoever in his life? Or should I pass down the *legacy* my mother gave to me? The one when she told me that there are only two things you need in life:

* You need a GREAT Faith in GOD, and

* You need a GREAT Sense of HUMOR!

And that's the challenge she set before me on a daily basis. And that's the same challenge I'm offering Baby Jake today. It's the challenge to build his character.

KATHLEEN J. DOLAN

SO WHAT!

SO WHAT if you're short.
SO WHAT if you're tall.
Not one of these things
Really matters at all!

SO WHAT if you're dark.
SO WHAT if you're light.
What matters is not
Your color or height!

SO WHAT—to these things!
They have no true meaning.
Your value derives
From your innermost being!

DAY 29

Focus daily on what really matters.

Thirty

Somehow, I figured out who it was.

OH SO ANNOYING!

Let's say my address was *17 Old Creek Road,* and it was on a busy main road. And let's say there was a tiny, offshoot street not far away with a similar address named: *17 Old Creek Lane.* Do you think this could cause any problems?

Little annoyances happen everyday, and we learn not to sweat the small stuff, right? So, when the mail from the other address kept coming to our house, I simply forwarded it back and didn't think anything of it. And when UPS packages continually were delivered—like a good neighbor—I patiently drove them over in my car and left them on the front porch of the folks at *17 Old Creek Lane.* Eventually, I introduced myself to the lady and she apologized for the inconvenience. Then, there were the frequent Pizza deliveries, and Chinese carryout deliveries, and I very cordially redirected the drivers to the correct address. Later, there were the four strange, cleaning ladies who walked into our house one day and started to clean! But what really annoyed me was when we woke up one morning and found a huge "dumpster" deposited in our driveway—*17 Old Creek Lane* was embarking on a large re-modeling project.

And so, again, we were the victims of a wrong delivery. But things weren't always bad. Twice, when I wasn't home, we had our entire lawn fertilized for FREE—their landscaping service messed up. And then I don't know how many times our home oil tank might have been filled-up either. Had a really good laugh once coming back from the grocery store—discovered that someone erected a giant, wooden STORK in our front yard! I knew I wasn't the one having a baby. Somehow, I figured out who it was.

Last fall we left our Connecticut home to vacation the entire winter in Florida. We hired a Home Check Service to watch over our house. One sunny morning, the Home Check Service phoned to inform us that there was a large, realtor's "FOR SALE" sign in front of our house.

Who do you suppose was moving?

KATHLEEN J. DOLAN

THIS TOO SHALL PASS

What does it matter
If the sink overflows?
Fifty years later
Nobody knows!

What does it matter
If your tires need air?
Fifty years later
Your car won't be there!

What does it matter
If your house goes to auction?
Fifty years later
You'll be in your coffin!

DAY 30

See all things in perspective.
"Don't sweat the small stuff!"

Thirty-One

KATHLEEN J. DOLAN

...the *joy* that was to follow...

THE POWER OF LETTING GO

Most women will admit to their joy at seeing their sons marry. Few will admit to their sense of loss.

Shortly before my younger brother was about to walk down the aisle, it was obvious to my sister and me that our mom was struggling with her feelings. Mom thought she was hiding it pretty well, but this was her baby and her only son, and it was really hard for her to see him leave. Naturally, she wanted only the best for him and all the happiness in the world—but she secretly mourned the fact that a special time in her life was about to pass away. Her baby had grown up!

Being a devout Catholic, my mother always had a devotion to the "Blessed Mother." So, I put myself in my mother's shoes, and composed a poem to "Mary," and then mailed it to her. Something very strange happened to me as I created this poem. I began to feel, in depth, all the sadness and pain my mother was going through, and it became even deeper than that as the poem unfolded. Tears streamed down my face and I cried out loud. But as the poem progressed, I saw the *joy* that was to follow, and in the matter of only a few minutes, the entire poem was written!

It would only be fitting to end these stories with this final poem. Any woman, of any faith, can relate to its universal feelings. It tells of *one Mother's profound love*:

"THE MOTHER OF THE GROOM!"

KATHLEEN J. DOLAN

"THE MOTHER of the GROOM"
(A Letter to Mary)

Dear Mother Mary,

How are you?
I hope you're doing fine.
I'd like to spend some time with you.
There's something on my mind.

My only son is leaving soon,
You see, he's just engaged.
The girl he's going to marry,
Is just about his age.

Now, I know I should be happy,
And pouring out the wine,
But way down deep inside me,
I want to keep him mine.

He's still my *little boy* you know.
I held him on my knee.
I watched him grow so fast and tall,
The handsome man you see.

He's been so great a joy to me,
How can I let him go?
The void that is to follow
Will surely be a blow.

(Continued)

Then—I think about that fateful noon,
The **CROSS**—before your eyes,
The only son you loved and held
Could barely hear your cries.

No—He wasn't being married
On an altar clean and bright,
But buried in a lonely tomb,
With dark, impending night.

It was a *Wedding* though,
That took place upon that day.
A Mother gave her Son,
In a *Marriage* bound to stay.

"He is the Groom; we are the Bride."
You held on to this view,
Then shared Him with the Whole World Wide,
Not keeping Him for *you.*

And Oh! The Joy you must have had
To see your "Precious Lamb,"
When Easter Morn He came to you,
And said, *"Mom, here I am."*

I guess you're right; we're much alike.
It's not all doom & gloom.
In many ways I'm just like you,
"The Mother of the Groom."

DAY 31

It's your turn now!
Write down your life stories, and...
"Share them with the Whole World!"

SUMMING IT ALL UP
(How to Give Yourself a Spiritual Face-Lift)

Here are some final thoughts to ponder on:

- Ironically, in the smallest and most ordinary circumstances, the greatest lessons often appear.

- Be on the outlook for these lessons.
  They have value, and must be told!

- As long as you are still breathing—you have the capacity to be *an Angel in the midst.* Your personal life stories can be shared with family, friends, the people you work with—and complete strangers!

So write down your own stories with the spiritual insights that you have learned. And when you are finished sharing them—see what comes back to you!

BOOMERANG!

P.S…Anyone for Chocolate?

A good friend is priceless!

KATHLEEN J. DOLAN

ACKNOWLEDGMENTS

It was no coincidence when I met a lady named Carol Stanley in 2002. Through her very special friendship, the stories in this book were brought forward. During an extended period of correspondence, we emailed our deepest thoughts, feelings, ideas, and emotions; we shared the gamut of experiences, and memories. Because of those personal exchanges, this *book of inspiration* was born. Carol is the catalyst that brought it all to light. She has been a compelling influence in my life—an honest, enlightening force— a genuine FRIEND!

FRIENDS

We have friends for a reason,
And friends for a season,
And friends who stay with us forever.

We have friends that are fun,
Some old and some young,
And we like them because they're so clever.

But the friends that we keep,
Are the friends that we meet,
Who stay with us through all kinds of weather.

They're the friends, who are true,
When we're happy or blue,
They're our friends when it's good, bad, or better!

ACKNOWLEDGMENTS

ALL PRAISE and THANKSGIVING goes to the Devine Spirit and the "Doctor of all Doctors" who created me—**GOD**.

As in all writing projects, this book was the result of many people's kind support, encouragement, and input. I want to extend my personal thanks and sincere appreciation to the friends and volunteers of my Reading Panel:
Carol Hammond, Kathy Jensen, Sharon Lewis, Kathy Mermey, Linda Pressman, and Sheryl Reifler,

A special thank-you to the **Rev. Matthew Calkins** for taking the time out of his busy schedule to personally offer his expertise and valuable suggestions. Thank You!

Thank You—to the two very knowledgeable people whose editorial help saved me from mutilating the English language—**Sharon Foster and Laura Pistey.**

A note of deep appreciation to my creative and poetic neighbor, **Anne Fasanella**, who served as cheerleader, offered remarkable editorial advice, and gave enthusiastic encouragement.

Let me give a loud applause to the staff and services of the **Westport Public Library** (Connecticut) for rendering such professional service—and kind, generous help.

My deepest THANKS to author, **Dale Carnegie**, whose books have so greatly enriched my life.

To my immediate family—words cannot express my gratitude for your unconditional LOVE—and most of all, to the man who has always been there for me, my husband **"Ken."**

ABOUT KATHLEEN J. DOLAN

Kathleen J. Dolan is a New York actress and comedienne who takes her greatest pleasure in speaking. She delights an audience with positive humor and spiritual wisdom.

With a unique ability to squeeze sense out of non-sense—she bonds with people on a heart to heart basis—which is so evident in her writing. Using innate humor, in the subtlest way, Kathleen gives inspiration and direction for creating a significant life. She credits her background as a trainer with the Dale Carnegie Organization as a major factor in giving her a personal vision. She is a genuine encourager and spiritual mentor.

If you would like to comment on this book, learn how to order additional books, know more about Kathleen's speaking schedule, or how to arrange for speaking engagements—contact her website address:

www.kathleenjdolan.com

Notes

KATHLEEN J. DOLAN